BITCOIN
AND DIGITAL
CURRENCY
for Beginners

THE BASIC LITTLE GUIDE

ALEX NKENCHOR UWAJEH

Bitcoin and Digital Currency for Beginners

The Basic Little Guide

By

Alex Nkenchor Uwajeh

The Basic Little Guide

Legal Notice:

The Basic Little Guide

Introduction

The emergence of digital currency has caused some disruption in the financial world, especially relating to the future of entire economies. Yet to the average person, the whole idea of a virtual currency existing only over the internet seems implausible. After all, if something doesn't exist in the form of physical coins or notes, how can it possibly be considered real currency?

What most people overlook is the money they spend from their own regular banking accounts on a daily basis also only exists on their bank's computer systems. Your salary might be credited directly into your bank, where the figure available is shown as a set of digital numbers. Likewise, the money you borrow from your bank for a mortgage or personal loan is actually a set of digital figures transacted from your account to the seller's account on a virtual system.

The Basic Little Guide

Believe it or not, this type of 'virtual' banking has been prevailing since the rapid rise of the fractional banking system several centuries ago. Think about it: does every bank in the world actually carry the amount of cash required to pay all of its depositors if they all stormed in on the same day and demanded their money?

Of course not. Banks carry only a small percentage of the actual amounts required for withdrawals. However, banks are able to lend money based on funds created using the virtual fractional banking system.

As the fractional banking system has been around for a few centuries now, nobody really blinks an eye at the idea of virtual currency in those terms.

Yet when you introduce them to the idea of virtual digital currency, a new level of skepticism emerges.

Are You Already Using Digital Transactions?

In recent decades, the idea of paying for items using digital payment processors, such as Paypal, has become more widely accepted by more people.

When you transact via an online payment processor, the figures you enter exist only as digital currencies. If you sell an item online via an ecommerce site, such as eBay, the buyer deposits digital currency into your Paypal account. You are then able to use that digital currency to purchase other items elsewhere. The virtual amounts of money only ever become real when you withdraw those amounts into your own bank account and then access them via a local ATM. Only then does the money shift from virtual to become real, physical currency.

As more people become familiar with digital transactions, the number of people using them has increased exponentially. Many traditional banks now prefer their customers to take advantage of online banking to view their balances or make digital transactions.

Of course, when you make a transaction online using digital technology, you're still dealing with real currency. You're just using digital technology to access funds.

By comparison, digital transactions aren't even close to the same thing as digital currencies.

The Basic Little Guide

What is Digital Currency?

Virtual currencies were developed in response to an overwhelming lack of trust with large financial institutions and fear surrounding digital transactions between banks.

The first real digital currencies were created to be completely independent of regular banks. A group of software programmers created the first digital currency, known as Bitcoin, in 2008. It was developed as a way to try and remove power from governments and big central banks in an effort to return some control over their own money back to the people.

In essence, when you use digital currency you aren't identified by name, allowing for a level of anonymity. Every transaction conducted is still recorded into a public ledger, which is known as a block chain. Each transaction is viewable by everyone, although the person associated with the transaction isn't readily identified. Instead, the transaction is linked to a server address to identify users.

It's important to note that there are three different terms used to describe digital currencies. Most people use all three terms to cover the same thing, yet there are subtle differences between them. These are:

Virtual currency: virtual currency is a specific type of unregulated digital money that is controlled by its developers. It operates in the same way as traditional money, allowing you to buy items or receive payments in virtual currency, but it doesn't have any physical or legal tender and is not issued by any central authority.

Digital currency: digital currency is a type of virtual currency that is created and transacted electronically, but is not issued by any central authority.

Crypto-currency: crypto-currency is a type of digital currency that is encrypted using cryptography to give it an increased level of security. The cryptography used makes it very hard to counterfeit, which generally makes it a safer form of digital currency.

How Does Digital Currency Work?

Digital currency works in much the same way as traditional currency. You're able to pay for items you purchase and you can receive payments for products or services. You're able to make payments to other people based purely on their address, rather than paying directly to an individual.

The digital currency remains in your digital wallet until you use it to pay for products or services, or until you exchange your virtual currency for traditional cash.

The Basic Little Guide

Each transfer or transaction of digital currency is recorded in the block chain ledger, which is essentially facilitated by a big network of computers using the same digital currency software. As each instantaneous transaction happens, it is verified and added to the block chain ledger.

Most digital currencies use a system known as 'mining' to help maintain their block chain. Individual computers running the required software are used to help process and verify transactions as they occur. Those individual computer users are known as miners, and they are rewarded with units of virtual currency for participating in the community and maintaining the block chain.

In the case of Bitcoin, the promise of earning more virtual currency by mining is now almost non-existent for individual users through personal computers now. Only those running upgraded computers with massive processing capacity or those running through large mining pools are able to benefit from earning or 'mining' new Bitcoins.

Fortunately, there are plenty of other digital currency alternatives to choose from that offer attractive incentives.

Bitcoins

Everyone is raving about Bitcoins, but not everyone knows what Bitcoins are or how to use them.

Here you will discover a world that allows you to transfer and store money in a safe and secure manner that is quick and inexpensive. You can manage your Bitcoins from anywhere in the world, and the only person you need to rely on is yourself.

This book will provide you with an insight into what Bitcoins are and where they came from. It will explain to you how Bitcoins can be used, where you can get them, and how Bitcoin compares to real money.

You will also discover how the Bitcoin process works, so that you can get your own wallet started. From downloading the software, to obtaining and using an address, you will discover all there is to know about Bitcoin and digital currency.

You will also be provided with information on mining, including what it means to be a Bitcoin miner and how you can become one. Most importantly, you will be given the tools you need to take a shot at using Bitcoins for yourself.

All your questions regarding Bitcoins and digital currency will be answered for you in a way that is easy to understand, helping you get started with digital currency.

The Basic Little Guide

Understanding Bitcoin

Although you may have heard the term
'Bitcoin' you may not know exactly what it
means. A bitcoin is simply digital currency,
also referred to as cryptocurrency. It can be
sent from one person to another via the
internet.

Bitcoins cannot be touched or placed into your
wallet. All cryptocurrencies are digital only.
This means that bitcoins only exist in
computers across the Bitcoin network, which
you can access by installing the Bitcoin
software onto your computer or by using an
online Bitcoin service.

You should consider Bitcoin to be cash used
on the internet, or internet cash. This means
that you can use the Bitcoins to buy products
or services, and receive Bitcoins in exchange
for products and services. You cannot deposit
Bitcoins into a regular bank account.

These transactions can only be done through the Bitcoin network. In order to start using Bitcoins and the Bitcoin network, you will need to download a Bitcoin client to your computer or sign up for an online network. You will learn more about that later on.

Bitcoins and Gold

For now, let's discover where Bitcoins originated.
Back in the days of the Great Depression gold was money and President Franklin Delano Roosevelt declared in an executive order that no one person could have more than $100 of gold. If you had more than $100 in gold, you had to turn it into the Federal Reserve banks. Failure to do so could result in being incarcerated for up to ten years.
The moral of the story is that government controlled the money. They confiscated what little gold the people had, then increased the

price of gold and used what they confiscated to increase their own bank accounts.

Taking lessons from history, a group of researchers, or perhaps just one man, decided to create a currency that was not under the control of the government, or any one specific organization. The goal is to create a form of money that the government could not profit from, but that individuals can use to purchase goods and services.

It all began with a man – or a pseudonym for a man or group of researchers – called Satoshi Nakamoto. No one really knows for sure if the person is a person or a group of people. What they do know is that a paper was written about these 'Bitcoins' and was then posted to a cryptography email list. This group or person had never used this email list before and no one using the list had ever heard of this person or group.

The Basic Little Guide

A few months later, software known as Bitcoin 0.1 was released to the same email list. After posting a few more times over the next few months, Nakamoto disappeared never to be seen or heard from again. However, he – or they – had created much buzz about this topic on discussion forums and the idea grew from there.

These decentralized, anonymous, electronic currencies have no regulatory authority controlling them. This is exactly the opposite of gold during the Great Depression, and US dollars and coins now, as well as other currencies across the world.

The rules and laws surrounding Bitcoins are built into the Bitcoin software.
Now, because there is no regulatory or government agencies controlling Bitcoins and the Bitcoin network, you may be wondering if the use of Bitcoins is legal. The answer is yes. Although governments and regulatory

agencies are conducting inspections into the use of Bitcoins and the Bitcoin network, the use of them is currently legal in the United States, and many other countries.

Where Can Bitcoins Be Used?

Bitcoin itself is not technically currency, as you have learned, but once it becomes more widespread, it will be. As for now, it is considered 'currency' as it can be exchanged online for both products and services.

Not only are there a growing number of stores online that accept Bitcoins, but there are also a few high street stores that do as well. Some large retailers accept Bitcoins in exchange for their goods.

If you are looking for an online spot that allows you to use Bitcoins relatively easily, you will want to head to Bitcoinin.com. It is similar to Amazon.com, offering a large variety of products.

Bitcoins versus Traditional Currencies

One of the biggest concerns with Bitcoins is how they differ from paper currencies. The concept behind the creation of Bitcoins is to avoid the government taking control. However, the problem with this is that the security and safety of Bitcoins is not guaranteed.

On the upside, retailers are finding that they get paid faster and with less fuss by accepting Bitcoins than they do with credit cards. This is what could put Bitcoins slightly ahead of cash.

Protecting Your Bitcoin Wallet

Bitcoins are a very secure means of buying and selling goods. With that said, if you lose your Bitcoins, you will equally lose all the addresses and private keys that you have stored. It is important that you keep a backup copy of your information as a preventative measure.

In order to protect your wallet from theft, you do want to secure it. This can be done by storing a copy of your wallet on an external devices, updating it as at when necessary and make sure you use an up to date and effective anti virus software. You can also add additional layer of protection to your Bitcoin wallet with the use of encryption.
The transaction fee for Bitcoin is relatively small and this is an added bonus.

Another advantage to using Bitcoins is that the transaction is not reversible and there is no middleman.

As with all types of currencies, there are a few downsides. First, changing between other types of currency and Bitcoins is not an easy process. You will learn more about how to change local currency into Bitcoins later, but a brief overview is that it just isn't easy.

Furthermore, transactions using Bitcoins are not instant, as they are with credit cards. Bitcoin transaction has to pass through the entire Bitcoin network to become validated, which does take some time.

Now that you know the advantages and disadvantages of using Bitcoins, you may be wondering if they are worth the hassle. While this decision is a personal one, consider the following to help make your decision easier:

- Your government has no control of Bitcoins / network and ownership is private. Money can equally be transferred to any part of the world.

The Basic Little Guide

The Bitcoin Process

Now that you know a little bit about what Bitcoins are, how they compare to local currency, and where you can use them, let's get started on how you can become a Bitcoin user.

Bitcoin Software and Address

The first step in becoming a Bitcoin user is to download the software which will create a Bitcoin wallet.

Similar to a bank account number, you do have a Bitcoin address that is specific to you. A sample address may look like this:

145JP9y8JZ7AyQfCJ7KFSBb1NBPwDZU HEY

The Basic Little Guide

With an address like this, no one will know who owns the address. Each transaction is recorded on every computer that is part of the Bitcoin network. This is referred to as a Block Chain. The Block Chain ensures that each and every transaction is legitimate.

In order to make a transaction happen, you will need to give out your address to the other person. It allows the buyer or seller to know where to send the money or where the money is coming from.

Mining, Verification and Blocks
Transactions must be verified by miners before completion and this could sometimes take longer depending on the scale of transactions.
However, in larger transactions, some sellers may await further confirmations from the Bitcoins network.

The Basic Little Guide

Bitcoin miners use their computer programming skills to help keep the network secure, create new Bitcoins and manage the processing of transactions on the Bitcoins network and they are rewarded with free 25 Bitcoins.

You have read the term Block or Block Chain several times throughout this book, and it is time to go a little more in depth about the topic, especially since it is important to mining and miners, not to mention a Bitcoin transaction.

A block is essentially a group of completed, verified transactions that have occurred over a period of time. Following that specific period of time, miners will use mathematical formulas and create what is referred to as a hash. This is a sequence of random numbers that protects the block from being altered.

A transaction that has been completed, verified, and entered into the block cannot be changed, altered, reversed, or modified in any way ever.

Turning Cash Into Bitcoins

Although the process of obtaining Bitcoins is complicated, there are many ways you can go about doing so. Once you have your wallet in place, you will need to go to a currency exchanger to complete the process.

Prior to choosing where to purchase your Bitcoins, it is recommended that you do some research. You want to make sure the company, the seller, and the website are legitimate. There can never be more than 21 million Bitcoins in existence.

Bitcoin Miner

Although the process of mining has already been explained, as well as the reward received by miners, you may be wondering how you can become a part of mining, or what is referred to as a miner.

In order to become a miner, you need to have specific mining hardware, which can cost anywhere from several hundred to several thousands of dollars. In addition, the cost of your electricity bill will greatly increase.

With that said, for beginners, it is best to join a group of Bitcoin miners who all work together and then split or share the profits.

The Basic Little Guide

Choosing Bitcoin Software

There are several different types of Bitcoin software and each one is different in the features that it offers and the level of difficulty to use them.

Bitcoin QT

The original Bitcoin client is Bitcoin QT and was developed by the mysterious Satoshi Nakamoto. All other Bitcoin clients are modeled after Bitcoin QT.

Other Desktop Clients

You can choose whichever desktop client you prefer, but it is a good idea to know what you are looking at.

Armory offers advanced features, which allows you to run several different wallets and can provide you with paper backups of your private keys. In addition, it allows you to store your Bitcoins on a separate computer that is offline. In order to use this software, however, you do need to have Bitcoin QT installed on your computer.

Electrum is another Bitcoin desktop client, but is slightly different from the other two. It does not require you to fully download the software to your computer and essentially runs online for the most part, using remote servers that have copies of the block chains while your wallet is still stored on your own computer.

MultiBit is similar to Electrum, as it does not require you to download the full program to your computer. In addition, it is available in a variety of different languages, which allows you to deal with those who do not speak English.

The Basic Little Guide

Online Wallets

As was mentioned earlier, you can opt to use a completely online wallet, which is referred to as an eWallet. It is faster to get started using an online wallet than it is to use a desktop wallet. This is because you are not required to download the software. Similar to desktop clients, there are several different types of online wallets.

Blockchain (Wallet) is perhaps the most advanced and secure online wallet you can choose in the Bitcoin world. Your wallet is encrypted and can only be accessed by you through your browser. Not even Blockchain administrators have the ability to access your wallet. It also includes features, such as automatic email or text notifications when you receive Bitcoins.

Does It Have to Be Bitcoin?

There are several different types of digital currencies for example: Litecoin, Dogecoin, Worldcoin and Feathercoin – Just to mention a few.

Litecoin

Litecoin is easily Bitcoin's biggest rival on the digital currency market. Litecoin is a cryptocurrency created by Charles Lee in 2011 as a nearly-identical replica of Bitcoin – with a few major differences. It's designed to work in much the same way as Bitcoin, but Litecoin features an open-source program to allow for more enhanced security of the network.

Another major difference between the two major virtual currencies is that Litecoin offers faster processing to the block chain. The current processing block time is logged at 2.5 minutes, as compared to Bitcoin's 10 minutes,

The Basic Little Guide

which means Litecoin is able to handle a much higher volume of transactions. Remember, the transaction is still instant. It's only the transaction verification time to the block chain we're talking about here.

Litecoin also uses the Scrypt proof-of-work algorithm, as compared to Bitcoin's SHA-256. The Scrypt proof-of-work algorithm incorporates the original SHA-256 algorithm, but produces calculations that are more highly serialized.

Perhaps the most notable difference between the two major digital currencies is that it's now impossible for a home user to mine Bitcoins on a home PC, while you can put your regular home computer's CPU to good use mining Litecoins to help add to your account. Miners are currently able to earn 50 new Litecoins per block.

The Basic Little Guide

Getting Litecoins

In order to get started, you will need a Litecoin wallet in order to store your Litecoins. All the wallets available contain encryption coding that allows you to view any of your transactions or check your account balance at any time, but requires that you enter your password before you spend any Litecoins from your account. This helps to protect your Litecoin wallet against viruses or trojans trying to steal from you.

There are several wallets available to download, including:

Desktop Wallets: you can download a wallet to your desktop PC, as Litecoin offers wallets for Windows, GNU/Linux and Mac OS.

Mobile Wallets: you can download a wallet to your Apple iPhone or your Android or Blackberry mobile device. The mobile wallet lets you scan QR codes for items you want to buy or tap your phone to pay for items at participating outlets.

Web Wallets: a web wallet allows you to transact using a web-based third-party wallet provider.

Once you have your wallet ready, there are three ways to get Litecoins.
- You can buy them on any of the cryptocurrency exchanges using traditional currency.
- You can accept payments in Litecoins for products or services.
- You can exchange other cryptocurrencies for Litecoins
- Or you can mine for Litecoins using your computer.

The Basic Little Guide

Mining Litecoins

It's very possible to increase your Litecoin balance by mining for Litecoins. The current reward is set at 50 Litecoins per block mined. You can use your computer's CPU (central processing unit) or your GPU (graphics processing unit).

You will need to download a free mining script that allows you to use your computer's processor to mine for Litecoins. Depending on your computer's operating system, you may need to configure the software to suit your needs. The precise settings you need will depend largely on your computer's graphics card or central processing unit.

The more transactions your computer helps to verify and add to the block chain, the more Litecoins you're able to earn. Keep in mind that mining on your own with a single computer can often take quite a lot of

The Basic Little Guide

processing power. This has the ability to affect other operations on your computer while your processor is verifying transactions. In most cases, solo miners have upgraded computers with very large processing capacities.

You also have the option of joining a mining pool, where your computer becomes just one in a group of processing computers. As part of a pool, you're able to help verify more transactions to the block chain, giving you the potential to earn more Litecoins overall.

You earn your share of the Litecoin rewards with others from your pool, so the amount you're able to earn will depend on how many blocks your pool is able to process. Again, you will need to configure the software to suit your own graphics card or central processing unit, but being part of a mining pool makes it easier to mine without requiring a massively upgraded computer with huge processing capacity.

Investing in Litecoins

Of course, not everyone who uses Litecoins is using them for buying or selling products or services. There are people who invest in them simply to wait for the value of their Litecoins to increase, much like investing on the stock market.

As cryptocurrencies do have value, it's very possible to use them as investment vehicles. Speculative traders purchase digital coins while the value is trading at a relatively low value, with the intention of converting those digital coins back to traditional currency again once the values have risen sufficiently to represent a profit. The volatility in the cryptocurrency market allows for massive gains in value in a relatively short period of time.

The Basic Little Guide

For example, it was reported in Forbes magazine that investors who purchased $100 worth of Litecoins at the beginning of 2013 can now cash in their wallets to the tune of $30,000. Back in January 2013 the value of 1 Litecoin was $0.07 cents. By December 2013 it had risen to $23.

Of course, that same level of market volatility also has the potential to compound losses, so it pays to do some homework before jumping into the speculative trading arena.

The exchange rate of Litecoins fluctuates in much the same way as the stock market or the foreign currency exchange, and there are various factors that can influence their value at any time.

For example, at the time of this writing 1 Litecoin is valued at $9.889 US dollars. Alternatively, 1 Litecoin is valued at £5.8306 British pounds or €7.30752 Euros.

The Basic Little Guide

Investing in Litecoins while the price has fluctuated to a relatively low point could offer the potential to see big returns as the prices adjust again in the near future. There's also the potential to add to your investment portfolio by earning more Litecoins via mining.

If you already have Bitcoins in your virtual wallet, you can also purchase Litecoins with Bitcoins on the crypto-exchange. At this time, you can exchange 1 Bitcoin for 61.9743 Litecoins.

Foreign Exchange Benefits

There's also the additional benefit of exchanging Litecoins for alternative currencies. Many investors love the idea of trading on the foreign currency exchange. Yet the spread many trading platforms place on the currency pairings means you may not always get the best value for your currency.

The Basic Little Guide

By comparison, investing one currency to purchase Litecoins and withdrawing cash in a different currency offers the potential for greater returns.

For example: You buy 10 Litecoins for $98.89 US dollars. That same value can be converted to £58.30 British pounds or €73.08 Euros or $105.58 Australian dollars without the added cost of exchange eating into your cash.

Yet if you were to exchange $98.89 US dollars via the foreign currency exchange on a forex trading platform or even electronically via your regular bank, you would receive much less on the exchange for your cash.

The example below shows the difference in exchange rate between Litecoins and exchanging traditional currency via Travelex:

The Basic Little Guide

Litecoin Value	US Dollar	British Pound	Euro	Australian Dollar
Litecoin	$98.89 USD	£58.30 GBP	€73.08 EUR	$105.58 AUD
Travelex	$98.89 USD	£54.08 GBP	€67.42	$102.44 AUD

If you're in a situation where you need to pay for products or services using foreign currencies, you actually get better value on the exchange through Litecoins. Foreign exchange platforms actually pay you slightly less when converting one currency to another, simply due to the spread they place between the prices of currency pairs. You don't have the additional cost of currency spread when exchanging Litecoins.

The Basic Little Guide

(Calculations correct as of June 2014, based on information available from http://litecoinexchangerate.org/, https://mcxnow.com/exchange/LTC and http://www.travelex.com.au/AU/Currency-Converter/)

Dogecoin

Dogecoin is the world's third most traded crypto-currency. It was created by Billy Markus in Portland, Oregon, and launched in December 2013. He created it in an effort to reach a much broader audience than Bitcoin reached.

The initial reaction to the release of Dogecoin was overwhelmingly positive, with Dogecoin community members raising enormous amounts of money to sponsor specific sporting teams. As an example, the Dogecoin community raised around $55,000 to sponsor NASCAR driver, Josh Wise. They also raised enough funds to help the Jamaican bobsled team get to the 2014 Winter Olympics.

For those considering investing in Dogecoins, the current price sits $1 US dollar for 2,783.29 Dogecoins. You're also able to exchange Bitcoins for Dogecoins.

At this time, 1 Bitcoin will buy you 1,694,915.25 Dogecoins. Alternatively, you can exchange 1 Litecoin for 26,301.45

You can also mine for Dogecoins to boost your account balance. Miners have the opportunity to earn around 125,000 Dogecoins for each block chain mined solo, as compared to earning 50 per block with Bitcoin. There are also plenty of active mining pools available for potential miners to join.

The Basic Little Guide

Worldcoin

Another prominent cryptocurrency available on the digital currency market is Worldcoin. The developers of this digital currency have been very proactive in promoting their currency and have a large list of e-commerce enable business websites that will accept Worldcoin as payment.

Worldcoin also uses scrypt hashing algorithms to verify transactions, which means it can also be mined in much the same way as Litecoin or Feathercoin. However, the big difference with Worldcoin is that their verification time is aimed at processing in 30 second blocks.

Compare this to the 2.5 minute block times for Litecoin and Feathercoin, or the 10 minute block times for Bitcoin, and you'll see it's designed to be a much faster system.

Miners have the opportunity to earn around 33 Worldcoins for each block chain mined solo. There are also plenty of active mining pools available for potential miners to join.

For those considering investing in Worldcoins, the current price sits at $0.016 USD for 1 Worldcoin. You are able to purchase Worldcoins using Bitcoins.

At this time, 1 Bitcoin will buy you 37,556.475 Worldcoins. Alternatively, you can exchange 1 Litecoin for 596.07 Worldcoins.

Feathercoin

Feathercoin could be considered one of the closest digital currencies to the original Bitcoin. It's mined in a very similar manner and the system functions along the same lines as Bitcoin, but it uses a scrypt-based algorithm much like Litecoin.

The Basic Little Guide

The primary difference with Feathercoin is that miners have the opportunity to earn 80 Feathercoins for each block chain mined solo, as compared to earning 50 with Bitcoin. There are also plenty of active mining pools available for potential miners to join.

Feathercoin also aims at a block chain verification time of 2.5 minutes, as compared to Bitcoin's 10 minutes per block.

One significant concept Feathercoin introduced is their Advanced Checkpointing system, which creates a central node for transactions to be monitored. This reduces their vulnerability to attack from major miners. It also helps to guard the system against other potential security vulnerabilities.

The larger supply of newly-created Feathercoins may also be more attractive to miners. The faster processing times and higher level of supply makes it much easier to earn more from your mining efforts.

For those considering investing in Feathercoins, the current price sits at $0.04977 USD for 1 Feathercoin. You're also able to exchange Bitcoins for Feathercoins.

At this time, 1 Bitcoin will buy you 12,434.5549 Feathercoins. Alternatively, you can exchange 1 Litecoin for 196.59 Feathercoins.

Take the time to review each of the options that are available and choose what works the best for you.

The Basic Little Guide

The Future of CryptoCurrency

When millions of people ventured into the online world of the internet two decades ago, critics said it would collapse as nothing more than a passing fad. Yet history has shown us that the internet really isn't going away any time soon.

Fast forward two decades and critics are now saying the future of cryptocurrency is just as bleak as the original emergence of the internet. And yet the digital currency exchanges are trading massive volumes of cryptocurrency daily, and are still growing in popularity.

Digital currency is emerging as a truly global currency unit that allows users to transfer something of value to another person without middlemen, such as banks, taking their share of the transaction. Asset holders are able to trade their digital currencies directly via decentralized exchanges that also cut out the middlemen, such as brokers.

The entire digital currency arena is still in its infancy, but it's sure maturing quickly. The technology behind cryptocurrency may only allow for the transfer of ownership of digital coins from one account to another right now. However, the technology also offers the scope to transfer ownership of any other kind of financial asset in future.

As more digital currencies enter the market, they bring with them even more advance technological innovations. As an example, Mastercoin is planning to release software that enables users and account holders to trade in other financial assets, such as stocks and bonds, along with other financial instruments and contracts.

It seems the future of cryptocurrency is destined to move from strength to strength as time passes. Will you be a part of the digital currency revolution?

Summing It Up - Bitcoins

Although there is a lot to Bitcoins and the Bitcoin network with all the addresses, wallets, security, miners and mining, and more, it may seem a little overwhelming. This book describes Bitcoins, Bitcoin software, and the Bitcoin network in basic, easy to understand language.
With the knowledge this book has provided, you now have a basic understanding of what Bitcoin is, where it came from, and how it works.

Warning: Prior to choosing where to purchase your Bitcoins, it is very important that you do some research. You want to make sure the company, the seller, and the websites are legitimate.

Your capital is at risk when you invest in Bitcoins and other crypto currencies - you can lose some or all of your money, so never risk more than you can afford to lose. Always seek professional advice if you are unsure about the suitability of any investment. Past performance is not a reliable indicator of future results.

Every attempt has been made to provide accurate, up to date and reliable complete information, no warranties of any kind are expressed or implied. Readers acknowledge that the author is not engaging in rendering legal, financial or professional advice.

The reader agrees that under no circumstances are we responsible for any losses, direct or indirect, which are incurred as a result of use of the information contained within this book, including – but not limited to errors, omissions, or inaccuracies.

The Basic Little Guide

Other Useful Resources

CoinDesk - Bitcoin News and Prices

CoinMarket – Buy and Sell Crypto Currencies – Bitcoins, Litecoins, Worldcoin, Feathercoin, etc

CoinBase – Buy and Sell Bitcoins

BlockChain – For wallets, charts and view transactions

BitCointalk - Forum

FeatherCoin – Forum

The Basic Little Guide

Check Out Other Books:

Investing in Gold and Silver Bullion - The Ultimate Safe Haven Investments

Nigerian Stock Market Investment: 2 Books with Bonus Content

The Dividend Millionaire: Investing for Income and Winning in the Stock Market

Economic Crisis: Surviving Global Currency Collapse - Safeguard Your Financial Future with Silver and Gold

Passionate about Stock Investing: The Quick Guide to Investing in the Stock Market

Guide to Investing in the Nigerian Stock
Market

Building Wealth with Dividend Stocks in the
Nigerian Stock Market (Dividends -
Stocks Secret Weapon)

Beginners Basic Guide to Investing in Gold
and Silver Boxed Set

Beginners Basic Guide to Stock Market
Investment Boxed Set

Precious Metals Investing For Beginners: The
Quick Guide to Platinum and Palladium

The Basic Little Guide

Taming the Tongue: The Power of Spoken Words

Beginners Quick Guide to Passive Income: Learn Proven Ways to Earn Extra Income in the Cyber World

Christian Living: 2 Books with Bonus Content

Thank you for downloading the book, Bitcoin and Digital Currency for Beginners:

The Basic Little Guide

The Basic Little Guide

If you would like to share this book with
another person, please purchase an additional
copy for each recipient. Thank you for
respecting the hard work of this author.

Bitcoin and Digital Currency for Beginners

The Basic Little Guide

Printed in the USA
CPSIA information can be obtained
at www.ICGtesting.com
LVHW012259120224
771703LV00008B/313

9 781507 787007